LET'S PLAY! LITTLE CHAMPS

CHEERLEADING

KIM THOMPSON

NorwoodHouse Press

Cataloging-in-Publication Data

Names: Thompson, Kim, 1970-.
Title: Cheerleading / Kim Thompson.
Description: Buffalo, NY : Norwood House Press, 2026. | Series: Let's play! little champs | Includes glossary and index.
Identifiers: ISBN 9781978577374 (pbk.) | ISBN 9781978577381 (library bound) | ISBN 9781978577398 (ebook)
Subjects: LCSH: Cheerleading--Juvenile literature. | Cheerleaders--Juvenile literature.
Classification: LCC LB3635.T474 2026 | DDC 791.64--dc23

Published in 2026 by
Norwood House Press
2544 Clinton Street
Buffalo, NY 14224

Designer: Rhea Magaro

Photo credits: Cover, p. 1 sirtravelalot/Shutterstock.com; p. 5 Dmytro Zinkevych/Shutterstock.com; p. 6 JoeSAPhotos/Shutterstock.com; p. 7 WoodysPhotos/Shutterstock.com; p. 8 Amy Myers/Shutterstock.com; p. 9 Shchus/Shutterstock.com; p. 11 Solomon Thompson/Shutterstock.com; p. 12 Amy Myers/Shutterstock.com; pp. 13, 14 Cherednychenko Ihor/Shutterstock.com; p. 15 Aleksei Lazukov/Shutterstock.com; p. 17 R-Tvist/Shutterstock.com; p. 18 PeopleImages.com - Yuri A/Shutterstock.com; p. 19 View Apart/Shutterstock.com; p. 21 Ground Picture/Shutterstock.com

Printed in the United States of America

TABLE OF CONTENTS

What Is Cheerleading?

Cheerleading is a fun sport. Cheerleading teams use strength and **flexibility** to dance, jump, and cheer. Their **stunts** and **formations** excite fans at sporting events.

The Uniform

Outfits made of stretchy fabric help cheerleaders move easily. Tops, skirts, and pants show the team colors.

Shoes must have good grip so that cheerleaders don't slip and fall.

A **ponytail** or bun keeps a cheerleader's hair out of the way. Hair ties and ribbons match the team colors. Bright, sparkly makeup helps cheerleaders stand out during performances.

The Field

At sporting events, cheerleaders perform on the **sidelines** to excite the crowd. During breaks in the game, they might do dances and stunts on the field.

COUGARS

Moves and Stunts

Cheerleaders practice many difficult moves. To do a high kick, they kick their legs high one at a time.

For a toe touch, cheerleaders spread their legs and touch their toes in midair.

To make a **pyramid**, some cheerleaders stand on the ground. Others are lifted up to stand on each other. Together, they form a pyramid shape.

For a basket toss, one cheerleader is the flyer. She gets tossed high in the air. The other cheerleaders catch her as she comes down.

Positions on the Team

Cheerleaders on a team have different jobs. Flyers get lifted and thrown into the air. They must be light and flexible.

Bases help lift the flyer up. They need to be strong and **steady**.

Spotters keep everyone safe. They stand near the bases. They catch flyers if they fall.

Front spotters watch the stunt from the front. Back spotters watch from the back.

How to Be Cheer-Ready

Cheerleaders should eat healthy foods like fruits, vegetables, and lean meats. They should drink plenty of water. Getting enough sleep gives them **energy** to perform at their best.

GLOSSARY

energy (EN-ur-jee): the ability to do work

flexibility (FLEK-suh-bil-i-tee): the ability to bend easily

formations (for-MAY-shuhnz): patterns, shapes, or arrangements

ponytail (POH-nee-tayl): a hairstyle that looks like a pony's tail in which the hair is pulled together and held with a band

pyramid (PIR-uh-mid): a shape with a polygon (such as a square) as a base and triangular sides that meet at a point on the top; things arranged to resemble a pyramid

sidelines (SIDE-lines): areas just outside the boundary lines of a court or field of play for a sporting event

steady (STED-ee): firm and stable; not shaky

stunts (stuhnts): acts that show great skill or daring

THINKING QUESTIONS

1. What does a cheerleader wear?
2. Why is the spotter an important position?
3. What do you think makes a pyramid difficult to perform?
4. Why do cheerleaders need to eat healthy foods?
5. What qualities do you think a good cheerleader has?

INDEX

ABOUT THE AUTHOR

Kim Thompson is a writer, mom, and sports fan from Columbus, Ohio. She loves to watch athletes' amazing skills on the court, field, or diamond. She believes that all kids should try out the sports that interest them and always remember to have fun!